Master Your CAREER With Vastu

Discover The Proven Path, Resolve 15 Career Dilemmas, Get Unstuck, and Find a Successful Profession That's Right for You.

Sooraj Achar

www.sooraj-achar.com

Copyright © 2023 by Sooraj Achar

All rights reserved.

No part of this book may be reproduced in any form without permission in writing from the author.

No part of this publication may be reproduced or transmitted in any form or by any means, mechanical or electronic, including photocopying or recording, or by any information storage and retrieval system, or transmitted by email or by any other means whatsoever without permission in writing from the author.

Your Free Gift !!

As a token of my thanks for taking out time to read my book, I would like to offer you a **Free-Gift**:

Scan Below **QR Code** to Download your **Free eBook PDF**.

Learn 395+ Mental Shift Words to Transform Your Performance in Every Area of Your Life - in the Next 30 Days!

You can also grab your **FREE GIFT** by typing in the below URL:

https://sooraj.sooraj-achar.com/free-gift

About Author

Sooraj Achar, Author of "**Master Your CAREER With Vastu**" - #1_BestSeller in USA, UK, India & Australia

Mr. Sooraj Achar was born in Bangalore, India. Growing up, he was fascinated with Mathematics, and his interest led to some early exposure to Numbers since he was drawn to stories related to Numerology.

Later, **Sooraj**, who is now a Software Engineer, developed a passion for **Numerology and Feng-Shui (Vastu)**. He is also a **Coach and Consultant**.

Being a Certified **Ho'oponopono & EFT Healer**, **Sooraj** explores the issues of How **Health, Relationships, Careers, & Money (HRCM)** can be Recognized, Transformed, and Navigated **toward a more Balanced, Harmonious, & Fulfilling Life.**

Sooraj loves to research **Human Psychology & Behavior** in order to get the maximum out of life. He is always eager to learn, embody, and then impart the fundamentals of optimal living to help others lead a resourceful life.

He is deeply convinced about the limitlessness of human potential and strongly believes that everyone has the potential to achieve more than one thinks about oneself.

MASTER YOUR CAREER WITH VASTU

Visit **www.sooraj-achar.com** to know more about his Life-Changing Book Catalogue.

https://amzn.to/3CgQHF9

https://medium.com/@soorajachar99

https://bit.ly/3M7gIu2

instagram.com/psychology_of_numberz/

https://bit.ly/3dO6aDh

https://bit.ly/3LXBTyz

https://bit.ly/3E9vKxc

• • • ● • ● • • •

Acknowledgements

How does a person say **"Thank You"** when there are so many people to thank?

Obviously, this book is a big thank you to my father **G Sathyanarayan Achar,** who is a powerful role model, and to my mother **G Pramila,** who taught me love and kindness.

My dearest ones most responsible for this book becoming a reality is my sister **Shruthi S,** brother-in-law **Saravana P,** and my cute niece **Naveeksha S.** They make my life complete.

Special thanks to my Mentor **Mr. Arvind Sood**, who taught me and guided me to become a **Numerology and Vastu - Coach & Consultant**.

Glad that I have been duly granted permission to use the words "Driver-Conductor" which is a creation of Mr. Arvind Sood.

I am grateful to **Mr. Som Bathla**, who is an Amazon **#1 Bestselling** author of multiple books; for mentoring, motivating, and guiding me to Write, Self-Publish, & Launch Books and for helping me start my **Author-preneur Journey.**

Last but not least, My Team: **Avesh Ansari(Profile), Akshay Bhat(work4ever24h), & Md. Bilal (Iconic_agency).**

• • • • • • • •

Dedication

This Book is Dedicated to My Grandparents,

R. Gangadharaiah & G. Vishalakshamma

And, My Dear Brother **Arvind Achar.**

• • • ● • ● • • •

Contents

How This Book Can Work Miracles in Your Life?   XIII

5 Key Takeaways from Each Chapter   XXV

1. Introduction to Commercial Vastu   1
2. Vastu For Schools, Colleges, And Educational Institutes   3
3. Vastu for Restaurant   7
4. Vastu For Salons/Parlor   11
5. Vastu For Factories   14
6. Vastu For Gym   27
7. Vastu for Boutique   30

8. Vastu for Petrol Pump	33
9. Vastu for Hospitals	36
10. Vastu for Cinema Hall & Theatre	39
11. Vastu for Banquet Halls	41
12. Vastu for Jewelry Shops	43
13. Vastu For Shops	45
14. Factory Location of ETP	49
15. Factories Location of Servant Quarters	51
Conclusion	54
May I Ask You for a Small Favor?	56
Preview of My Best Selling Books	59
Testimonials	71
Author Profile	78
Disclaimer	80

How This Book Can Work Miracles in Your Life?

Miracles in Your Life

I have seen miracles happen to men and women from all walks of life all over the world. Miracles will happen to you too when you begin using the magical power of your true potential. This book is designed to teach you How to Transform and Navigate your life through Feng-Shui/Vastu?

What Role Do Feng-Shui and Vastu Play in Your Life?

The term Feng Shui refers to air (Feng) and water (Shui). When someone frequently falls ill, we usually suggest changing their surroundings, such as going to a hill station or somewhere else for vacations. In China, people say that you need to do your Feng Shui, which means to change the water and air. Both these elements are critical in Feng Shui.

Relationship between Vastu and Feng-Shui:

Vastu is used to diagnose, and Feng Shui is the remedy. Vastu is used to identify the disease, and Feng Shui is the medicine. Vastu and Feng Shui are complementary to each other. They share a fundamental belief in the importance of creating a harmonious and balanced environment to support health, happiness, and prosperity. Both systems can be useful in helping individuals to create more harmonious and balanced living and working spaces.

Vastu and Feng Shui are both ancient systems of architecture and design that originated in different parts of the world but have similar aims to harmonize people with their surroundings.

Vastu Shastra is an ancient Indian science of architecture and construction, which is based on the principles of harmony and balance between humans and their environment. The main focus of Vastu is to create a harmonious balance between the five elements of nature, i.e., earth, water, air, fire, and space. It emphasizes on directions and orientation and uses various elements like colors, shapes, and materials to create a balance and positive energy in the living spaces.

Feng Shui, on the other hand, is a Chinese philosophical system of harmonizing everyone with the surrounding environment. It is based on the principles of Qi (Chi), the life force that flows through all living things, and Yin and Yang, the balance of opposite forces. Feng Shui focuses on the placement of objects, furniture, and structures in living spaces to optimize the flow of energy or "Qi." It also takes into consideration the orientation of the building, the placement of doors and windows, and the use of colors, shapes, and materials to create balance and harmony.

In summary, both Vastu and Feng Shui aim to create balance and harmony in living spaces, but Vastu is more focused on directions and orientation, while Feng Shui emphasizes the flow of energy and balance of opposing forces.

Here are some alternative forms of Vastu and its usage in different parts of the world:

1. **Sacred Space Design** - It is a design approach that focuses on creating spaces that are spiritually meaningful and facilitate connection with the divine, using principles of sacred geometry, symbolism, and ritual.

2. **Architecture** - It is the art and science of designing and constructing buildings and other physical structures.

3. **Space Planning** - It is the process of arranging and organizing interior spaces to make them functional and attractive.

4. **Sacred Geometry** - It is a belief system that asserts a spiritual significance to geometric shapes and mathematical principles.

5. **Environmental Design** - It is the process of creating and shaping the physical environment, including buildings, landscapes, and infrastructure, to meet human needs and improve quality of life.

6. **Geomancy** - It is an ancient divinatory practice that involves interpreting markings on the ground, such as patterns formed by stones or earth.

7. **Sthapatya Veda** - It is a traditional Indian system of architecture that focuses on creating buildings and structures in harmony with nature.

8. **Biophilic Design** - It is an approach to architecture and interior design that seeks to connect people with nature by incorporating natural elements and patterns into built environments.

9. **Permaculture Design** - It is a design system that integrates ecological principles and practices to create sustainable and regenerative human settlements.

10. **Landscape Architecture** - It is the design of outdoor spaces, such as parks, gardens, and public spaces, that integrates natural and cultural elements to create functional and aesthetically pleasing environments.

A Poem on Vastu:

In ancient times, our forefathers knew
The importance of spaces and energy too
!!

They created Vastu, a science so pure
To bring balance and harmony, that's for sure!!

A home that's aligned with Vastu's laws
Ensures happiness, health, and applause !!

The sun and wind, the water and earth
All come together to create a rebirth !!

East is the direction of the morning sun
The source of energy and vitality, that's no pun!!

North brings prosperity and wealth galore
While the south is the abode of Yama, God of the core !!

The kitchen should face southeast
To cook up a storm, and never to rest !!

The bedroom in the southwest, a space of peace
To rejuvenate the mind, and the body to ease !!

The living room in the northeast, where guests are welcomed
To bask in the warmth, and be enlightened !!

    The puja room in the center, a sacred place
To worship the divine, and seek grace !!

Vastu is more than just design
It's a way of life, that's so divine !!

    A connection to the universe, a cosmic bond
To live in harmony, and beyond !!

SOORAJ ACHAR

So let us all embrace Vastu's laws
And bring balance and harmony, that's no pause !!

Let our homes be a reflection of our souls
A space of love, peace, and goals.

• • • ● • ● • • •

Reason for Writing This Book

It is for the express purpose of answering and clarifying the above questions and many others of a similar nature that motivated me to write this book. I have endeavored to explain the great fundamental truths of your strengths and weaknesses in the simplest language possible. I believe that it is perfectly possible to explain the basic, foundational, and fundamental laws of life and your mind in ordinary everyday language.

You will find that the language of this book is used in your daily papers, in your business offices, in your home, and in the daily workshop.

I urge you to study this book and apply the techniques outlined therein; and as you do, I feel absolutely convinced that you will lay hold of a miracle-working power that will lift you up from confusion, misery, melancholy, & failure, and guide you to your true place, solve your difficulties, severe you from emotional & physical bondage, and place you on the royal road to freedom, happiness, and peace of mind.

This miracle-working Power of Directions can heal your weaknesses, make you vital and strong again, and navigate your life through Feng-Shui/Vastu.

• • • ● • ● • • •

5 Key Takeaways from Each Chapter

1. Key Takeaways from the chapter on Commercial Vastu:

1. Similar Principles: The basic principles of Vastu remain the same for commercial buildings as they do for residential properties. Whether it's a jewelry shop, factory, or petrol pump, the fundamental Vastu principles learned before still apply.

2. Common Locations: Locations such as the staircase, boring, underground tank, and toilets follow the same guidelines as discussed in residential Vastu. There is no

difference in Vastu principles for these common areas between residential and commercial properties.

3. Focus on Amenities: Commercial Vastu emphasizes the amenities specifically required in factories and commercial buildings. This chapter delves into these specific requirements to ensure optimal Vastu compliance for commercial spaces.

4. Factory Vastu: The chapter specifically addresses the Vastu considerations for factories. It provides insights into the Vastu aspects relevant to factory setups, highlighting the importance of aligning the space with Vastu principles for enhanced productivity and harmony.

5. Comprehensive Knowledge: By understanding commercial Vastu, readers gain a comprehensive understanding of Vastu principles that can be applied to different types of businesses. This knowledge enables individuals to make informed decisions when it comes to setting up commercial spaces in alignment with Vastu guidelines.

2. Key Takeaways from the chapter on Vastu for Educational Institutes:

1. Playground is Key: According to Vastu, the playground holds great importance in the design of educational institutes. A balanced and well-placed playground is crucial as it can have a positive impact on the overall functioning of the school.

2. Ideal Direction: The best directions for the playground are the East, Northeast (NE), and North. If the majority of the playground falls in these directions, it is believed to contribute to the success of the school. Conversely, having the playground in the West sector may diminish the possibility of success.

3. Openness and Energy: Keeping the East, NE, and North as open as possible is recommended in Vastu for educational institutes. These directions are considered origin points of energy. The building should be situ-

ated in the South, Southwest (SW), and West, as these directions have the capability to hold heavy weight.

4. Central Playground: Having the playground in the center and the building on the periphery of the plot is considered healthy in Vastu. It is advisable to keep the NE area as empty as possible. Additional features like water pools, boring, or submersibles can be constructed in the NE direction.

Extra Important Points:

1. Classroom Orientation: Students should face towards the East or North in the classroom, while the teacher should face towards the West or South.

2. Principal's Office: The principal's office should be located in the Southwest (SW) or South direction according to Vastu principles.

3. Canteen Placement: Canteens are recommended to be situated in the Southeast (SE) or Northwest (NW) directions for optimal Vastu compliance.

3. Key Takeaways from the chapter on Vastu for Restaurants:

1. Kitchen Location: The location of the kitchen is a crucial factor for the success of a restaurant. The recommended directions for building the kitchen are Southeast (SE), Northwest (NW), and East (E). Among these, NW is considered favorable as it is associated with the element of Air, which attracts guests. If NW is not possible, West and South can be considered as alternative positions.

2. Avoid Certain Locations: Building the kitchen in the North, Northeast (NE), Southwest (SW), or center of the restaurant is strongly discouraged. These locations are not conducive to a successful restaurant business, as discussed in detail in residential Vastu.

3. Color Combinations: Choosing the right colors for the restaurant plays a significant role in creating a positive ambiance. The recommended colors are yellow,

maroon, and white. Various combinations of these colors can be used to create an atmosphere that symbolizes success and prosperity.

4. Consider Other Vastu Factors: While kitchen location and color combinations are important, it is also essential to consider other Vastu principles discussed in "Residential Vastu" or "Master Your Growth With Vastu" for the design and layout of other rooms and utilities within the restaurant.

5. Overall Prosperity: While kitchen location and color combinations are key factors, it is crucial to recognize that overall prosperity and success in the restaurant business are influenced by a combination of various factors. Considering all aspects of Vastu and other business strategies is necessary for maximizing the chances of success in the restaurant industry.

4. Key Takeaways from the chapter on Vastu for Beauty Parlors and Unisex Salons:

1. Importance of Mirror and Wash Basin: The mirror and wash basin are key elements for the success of a salon. These are major attractions for customers, and their proper placement is crucial for profitability.

2. Recommended Positions: The best positions to install the mirror and wash basin are the walls in the Northeast (NE), East, and North directions. These directions are considered beneficial and extend the positive energy of the salon.

3. Avoid Other Directions: It is important to avoid installing mirrors and wash basins in any other direction apart from NE, East, and North. Installing them in other directions can lead to problems and losses in the business.

4. Color Composition: White is the ideal color choice for beauty parlors and salons. It is associated with Venus, which is considered the driving force for such businesses. While other colors can be used based on design and theme, incorporating white as much as possible is recommended.

5. Placement of Showcase/Window for Beauty Products: If the salon sells beauty products, it is advised to build the showcase, window, or shelf for these products in the Northwest (NW) direction. This placement can help increase sales of beauty products.

These key takeaways highlight the significance of the proper placement of mirrors, washbasins, color choices, and strategic placement of beauty products showcase in accordance with Vastu principles for creating a harmonious and successful environment in beauty parlors and salons.

5. Key Takeaways from the chapter on Vastu for Factories and Commercial Buildings:

1. Location of Machinery: The ideal locations for placing machinery in a factory are Southeast (SE), South, and West. These directions have the capability to hold heavy weight and are associated with earth elements. For lighter machinery, the West direction can be considered. Other directions should be avoided.

2. Consider Weight for Raw Material: Raw material in the factory should be stored in directions that can handle the weight. The recommended directions for raw material storage follow the same logic as the store room. If unavoidable, a platform 3-4 inches above the ground can be built in prohibited directions to allow airflow below the material.

3. Storing Finished Goods: Finished goods should be stored in directions that facilitate quick sales. The pre-

ferred directions for storing finished goods are Northwest (NW), North, and West. If stored in avoided directions, goods should be picked from NW, North, or West and used to fill the empty space in the avoided direction.

4. Owner's Office Location: The best locations for the owner's office in a factory are Southwest (SW), South, and West. If these directions are not available, other directions can be considered in sequence, except for the center. The office furniture should have legs, and the owner's chair should face North, East, or Northeast (NE).

5. Location of Boilers: Boilers without chimneys should be placed in SE, NW, or East directions. Boilers with chimneys should be located in SE, NE, or South, West, and East directions. Other directions should be avoided due to their negative impact on fire elements and energy balance.

These key takeaways emphasize the importance of proper direction and placement of machinery, raw material, finished goods, owner's office, and boilers in factories and commercial buildings according to Vastu principles. Adhering to these guidelines can contribute to a harmonious and successful working environment.

6. Key Takeaways from the chapter on Vastu for Gyms:

1. Placement of Fitness Equipment: The success of a gym relies heavily on its fitness equipment. Heavy equipment should be placed in the Southwest (SW), South, and West directions, as these directions can handle the weight. For medium-weight equipment, the Southeast (SE) and Northwest (NW) directions are suitable.

2. User Orientation: Position the gym equipment in such a way that users face North or East while using them. Avoid equipment facing South and West direc-

tions. This orientation aligns with the principles of energy flow and provides a more harmonious workout experience.

3. Mirrors: Mirrors are an essential element in gyms. The ideal locations for mirrors are the Northeast (NE), East, and North directions. These directions should not be compromised, as mirrors serve as important focal points and aid in creating a positive ambiance in the gym.

4. Color Combination: Choose colors such as white, maroon, blue, and green for the gym's interior. These colors promote a sense of positivity, energy, and freshness. However, it is advisable to avoid using black as it may create a heavy or negative atmosphere in the gym.

5. Consider Equipment as Weight: When designing the Vastu for a gym, it is important to consider the weight of the fitness equipment. Placing heavy equipment in appropriate directions and ensuring user orientation

and favorable colors can contribute to a successful and energizing gym environment.

These key takeaways highlight the significance of proper equipment placement, user orientation, mirror positioning, and color selection in creating a Vastu-compliant gym that supports the well-being and fitness goals of its users.

7. Key Takeaways from the chapter on Vastu for Boutiques:

1. Placement of Special Articles: If you have specific articles that you want to sell in maximum numbers for maximum profitability, place them in the Northwest (NW), West, and North directions. These directions are believed to enhance sales and attract customers.

2. Show Windows and Mannequins: Install your show windows and mannequins in the Southwest (SW) and South directions. These positions are considered suit-

able for attracting attention and showcasing your garments effectively.

3. Owner/Manager/Cashier Counter: The counter for the owner, manager, or cashier should be positioned in the Southwest (SW) or South directions. It is advisable to face North or East while working at the counter, as it aligns with positive energy flow and facilitates better financial transactions.

4. Trial Room: The best location for the trial room is in the West, followed by the South and SW directions. Avoid placing the trial room in the Northeast (NE) and East directions. The mirrors in the trial room should be placed on the walls in the North, East, and NE directions.

5. Tailor's Position: For the tailor's work area, the ideal locations are the South and Southeast (SE) directions. These directions are associated with Mars, which represents machine operation. Placing the tailor in these zones aligns with the energy of their work.

6. Color Combination: The ideal color combination for the boutique is green and white. Green, representing Mercury, symbolizes balance and prosperity, while white, representing Venus, is helpful for this business. Strive to keep green as the dominant color in your boutique's interior design.

By following these guidelines related to the placement of garments, trial rooms, show windows, mannequins, tailor positions, and color combinations, you can enhance the positive energy flow, attract customers, and create a harmonious and prosperous environment for your boutique.

8. Key Takeaways from the chapter on Vastu for Petrol Pumps:

1. Pit Placement: The key point of a petrol pump is the storage pits for petrol. The ideal directions for creating pits are Northeast (NE), East, and North. Placing pits in these directions is believed to contribute to the suc-

cess of the petrol pump. However, if the pits are located in the Southwest (SW), Southeast (SE), or South directions, it may result in significant losses for the business.

2. Alternative Pit Options: The West and Northwest (NW) directions are considered neutral options for pit placement. If the preferred directions are not feasible, these directions can be chosen as the last resort.

3. Consider Other Structures: In addition to the pits, it is important to build other structures such as boring areas, owner's cabins, and toilets according to Vastu principles. This holistic approach ensures positive energy flow and harmony within the petrol pump premises.

4. South-Facing vs. North-Facing: The belief that south-facing petrol pumps are bad and north-facing ones are good is not necessarily true. The success of a petrol pump depends on various factors. South-facing petrol pumps can thrive if the tank is located in the north, aligned with the entry direction of vehicles. On the other hand, north-facing petrol pumps can face

challenges because the tank would be in the south, which contradicts Vastu principles.

5. Factors and Safety Precautions: The positioning of petrol tanks in petrol pumps takes into account factors such as public safety. The direction of the petrol pump and the corresponding tank placement depends on the entry direction of vehicles and safety regulations rather than a strict north-facing or south-facing rule.

By considering the appropriate placement of pits, aligning with Vastu principles, and considering other aspects of the petrol pump structure, you can create a positive and conducive environment for the business.

9. Key Takeaways from the chapter on Vastu for Hospitals:

1. Importance of ICU, OT, and OPD: The success and reputation of a hospital largely depend on its Intensive Care Unit (ICU), Operation Theater (OT), and Out-

patient Department (OPD). These departments are considered the pillars of a hospital's reputation, with lower mortality rates contributing to a higher reputation.

2. Ideal Locations for ICU and OT: The best location for ICU and OT is the East, followed by the North, Northeast (NE), and finally the West. The East is associated with health and purity, while the NE is the purest direction. However, due to concerns about maintaining purity and avoiding construction in the NE, it is ranked third. The West, although impure, can still be a good direction for ICU and OT due to its energy flow from East to West.

3. Avoidance of South, Southwest, and Northwest for ICU and OT: It is important to avoid placing ICU and OT in the South and Southwest directions, as these are considered impure directions associated with Yama and Rahu-Ketu. These zones are considered dangerous for patients. The Northwest should also be avoided due to

its association with air, as excessive airflow can create potentially hazardous conditions.

4. Preferred Direction for OPD: The best direction for the OPD, where patients come for consultations and then leave, is the Northwest, followed by the North and West. These directions are believed to create a favorable environment for patient interactions and healthcare consultations.

5. Color Combination: The dominant color for hospitals is yellow or shades of yellow. Yellow represents healing and is associated with Jupiter, who is considered the Guru of Gods. Incorporating yellow into the hospital's color scheme can create a soothing and healing atmosphere. For doctors' cabins, the preferred directions are the Southwest, West, and South.

By considering the recommended locations for ICU, OT, and OPD, and incorporating the appropriate color combinations, hospitals can create a harmonious and conducive environment for patients, staff, and healthcare services.

10. Key Takeaways from the chapter on Vastu for Cinemas:

1. Screen Placement: The key point of a cinema is its screen, and the best directions to install the screen are the Northeast (NE), East, and North. Placing the screen in these directions ensures that viewers face these directions while enjoying the movie, creating a harmonious viewing experience.

2. Slope of Seats: The seats in the theater are arranged on a slope, with the first row at the lowest level and the last row positioned above all. This arrangement allows viewers in the last row to have a clear view of the screen. For better prosperity and success, the slope of the seats should be towards the NE, East, and North, aligning with the favorable directions for the screen placement.

3. Ticket Window Location: The ticket window, where tickets are sold, should be positioned in the Northwest (NW), West, or North directions. Placing the ticket window in these configurations is believed to enhance ticket sales and contribute to the overall success of the cinema.

4. Consideration of Prosperity and Success: The chapter emphasizes the importance of Vastu principles in promoting prosperity and success in cinemas. By aligning the screen placement, seat slope, and ticket window location with the recommended directions, it is believed that the cinema can attract more viewers and achieve greater success.

5. Implementation of Vastu Principles: By following the Vastu guidelines provided in the chapter, cinema owners and operators can create an environment that is conducive to a positive movie-watching experience. Proper positioning of the screen, seating arrangement,

and ticket window can contribute to the overall ambiance and success of the cinema.

Implementing these Vastu recommendations can help create a favorable and harmonious cinema environment, enhancing the viewers' experience and contributing to the overall success of the establishment.

11. Key Takeaways from the chapter on Vastu for Indoor Banquet Halls:

1. Stage Placement: The key point of an indoor banquet hall is its stage, and the ideal locations for the stage are the Southwest (SW), South, and West directions. These directions provide a strong and elevated position for the stage, which is considered beneficial. It is important to avoid placing the stage in the Northeast (NE), East, and North directions.

2. Consideration of Elevation and Robustness: The SW, South, and West directions are preferred for the

stage due to their elevated and robust qualities. A well-positioned and sturdy stage in these directions is believed to enhance the overall atmosphere and success of the banquet hall.

3. Facilities Design: In addition to the stage, other facilities in the banquet hall, such as toilets, staircases, and kitchens, should also be designed according to Vastu principles. Proper placement and alignment of these facilities contribute to the overall harmony and functionality of the space.

4. Separate Halls for Different Functions: In larger banquet halls, separate halls or sections are often designated for starters, the main course, and coffee. It is recommended to construct these halls in the SW, South, and West directions. Avoiding the NE, East, and North directions for these halls ensures that the energy flow remains favorable and aligned with Vastu principles.

5. Vastu for Overall Ambience: The chapter highlights the significance of Vastu principles in creating a harmo-

nious and auspicious environment in indoor banquet halls. By carefully considering the placement of the stage, facilities, and separate halls, banquet hall owners can enhance the overall ambiance, guest experience, and success of their establishment.

Implementing these Vastu recommendations can help optimize the layout and design of indoor banquet halls, ensuring an auspicious and harmonious environment for events and functions.

12. Key Takeaways from the chapter on Vastu for Jewelry Shops:

1. Safe Placement: The key point in a jewelry shop is safe where valuable items are stored. The ideal locations for placing the safe are the Southwest (SW), South, or West directions. These directions symbolize stability and are considered the best for the safe. It is important to avoid placing the safe in the Northwest (NW), Southeast (SE), East, and North directions. The

SE direction, although neutral, is not preferred for the safe.

2. Mirror Installation: Mirrors in a jewelry shop should be installed in the North, East, and Northeast (NE) directions. These directions are considered favorable for mirrors. However, it is important to avoid installing mirrors in all other directions. By adhering to these guidelines, the energy flow and aesthetics of the jewelry shop can be enhanced.

3. Owner's Seating: The seating arrangement for the shop owner is crucial. While dealing with customers and managing the shop, the owner should face the Northeast (NE), East, or North directions. These directions are considered the purest, and by aligning with them, the owner can benefit from the positive energy throughout the day. It is recommended to avoid facing other directions while sitting in the shop.

4. Significance of Stability: The chapter emphasizes the importance of stability in a jewelry shop. Placing the

safe in the SW, South, or West directions promotes a sense of security and stability for the valuable items stored in the shop. These directions are associated with grounding and solidity, making them ideal for the safe.

5. Vastu for Positive Energy: The application of Vastu principles in a jewelry shop aims to create a positive and harmonious environment. By aligning the placement of the safe, mirrors, and owner's seating with specific directions, the jewelry shop can attract beneficial energies and create an auspicious atmosphere for both the owner and customers.

Following these Vastu guidelines can help optimize the layout and design of a jewelry shop, ensuring a harmonious and prosperous environment for conducting business and enhancing the overall success of the establishment.

13. Key Takeaways from the chapter on Vastu for Various Shops:

1. Owner's Seating: The seating arrangement for the shop owner depends on the direction the shop faces. The recommended seating positions are as follows:

- South or West-facing shop: The owner should sit in the Southwest (SW) direction.

- North-facing shop: The owner should sit in the North or Northeast (NE) direction.

- East-facing shop: The owner should sit in the East or NE direction.

- Northeast-facing shop: The owner should sit in the North direction.

- Southeast-facing shop: The owner should sit in the South direction.

- Northwest-facing shop: The owner should sit in the West direction.

- Southwest-facing shop: The owner should sit in the South direction.

2. Important Stock Placement: The stock that the shopkeeper wants to sell in large quantities should be placed in the Northwest (NW), North, and West directions. These directions are believed to enhance sales and attract customers.

3. Cash Box Placement: The cash box should be positioned in a way that it opens toward the North, East, or NE directions. If that is not possible, using cash boxes with lids that can be opened directly upwards is recommended. It is important to avoid opening the cash box towards the South and Southwest directions, as per Vastu principles.

4. Temple Placement: If there is a temple in the shop, it should be built or installed in the Northeast (NE), East,

or North directions. These directions are considered auspicious for placing religious or spiritual items.

5. Color Combination: The color scheme for the shop should predominantly be white or off-white. It is advisable to avoid using dark colors, as they may create a heavy or negative ambiance.

Other Considerations:

- Avoid placing any goods in the center of the shop.

- The main gate of the shop should also be designed and positioned according to Vastu principles.

By implementing these Vastu guidelines, shop owners can create a positive and harmonious environment in their shops, which may potentially enhance business success, customer satisfaction, and overall prosperity.

14. Key Takeaways from the chapter on Vastu for Effluent Treatment Plants (ETPs):

1. Ideal Directions: The ideal directions for constructing an Effluent Treatment Plant (ETP) are the Northeast (NE), east, and north. These directions are considered favorable for water-related elements and activities due to the presence of water in the ETP.

2. Water Element: Since ETPs involve the treatment and recycling of large amounts of water, it is important to align the directions according to the water element. This helps to maintain a harmonious flow and balance within the ETP.

3. Digging and Water Storage: As the construction of an ETP requires digging and building tanks for water storage, the directions suitable for ETPs are similar to those recommended for boring, underground tanks,

and submersibles. These directions are believed to support efficient water management and storage.

4. Avoid Other Directions: It is advised to avoid constructing ETPs in directions other than the NE, east, and north. Other directions may not be suitable for maintaining the desired functionality and effectiveness of the ETP.

5. Government Water Supply: ETPs are commonly used in factories to recycle water as an alternative to relying solely on government water supply, which may not be sufficient for industrial needs. By implementing an ETP, factories can contribute to water conservation efforts while ensuring an adequate water supply for their operations.

By considering the Vastu guidelines for ETP construction, factories can optimize the functionality and efficiency of their treatment plants, promoting sustainable water management practices within their operations.

15. Key Takeaways from the chapter on servant quarters' ideal locations:

1. Best Location: The best and ideal location for servant quarters is the southeast (SE) direction. In ancient times, this direction was chosen to ensure that servants woke up early and completed most of their work before the employers woke up. The SE is associated with the fire element, providing energy and productivity to the workers.

2. Alternative Location: If the SE is not feasible, the next best location for servant quarters is the west direction. The West is considered a stable zone, fostering loyalty, trustworthiness, and compatibility between the workers and the employer.

3. Third Best Zone: The east direction is considered the third best zone for constructing servant quarters. While not as preferable as the SE or West, the east direction

can still be suitable for providing accommodation to workers.

4. Avoid Southwest and South: It is strongly advised to avoid constructing servant quarters in the southwest (SW) and south directions. These areas are associated with the owner's zone, and placing servant quarters there may lead to issues of jealousy or the workers aspiring to become owners.

5. Avoid Northwest, North, and Northeast: Additionally, it is recommended to avoid constructing servant quarters in the northwest (NW), north, and northeast (NE) directions. These directions may not be conducive to maintaining a harmonious and balanced living environment for the workers.

By considering these guidelines, factory owners can choose appropriate locations for servant quarters that promote a positive and productive living environment for their workers.

• • • • • • • • •

Chapter 1

Introduction to Commercial Vastu

"Feng Shui and Vastu are like gentle whispers guiding us to create harmonious spaces."

All our previous Books were on Residential Vastu. Now it's time to learn Vastu for your business. Commercial Vastu has received too much hype in the market, which is completely unnecessary. Suppose you want to check Vastu for a commercial building. It can be a jewelry shop, a factory, or even a petrol pump; the basic Vastu principles would be the same as what we have learned before.

In this chapter, we will discuss the Vastu of factories. However, I won't delve into the locations of the staircase, boring, underground tank, toilets, etc., because they are exactly the same as what we have discussed before. There is no difference between residential and commercial Vastu when it comes to these common locations. But why are we learning about commercial Vastu? It's because, in commercial Vastu, we focus on the amenities specifically required in factories and commercial buildings.

・・・●・●・・・

Chapter 2
Vastu For Schools, Colleges, And Educational Institutes

"Feng Shui and Vastu are like gentle whispers guiding us to create harmonious spaces."

In this chapter, we will learn about the things we need to remember while designing the Vastu of educational institutes.

The most important thing for a school, according to Vastu, is the playground. If the playground is balanced, it will manage all other things automatically. The playground is the key factor.

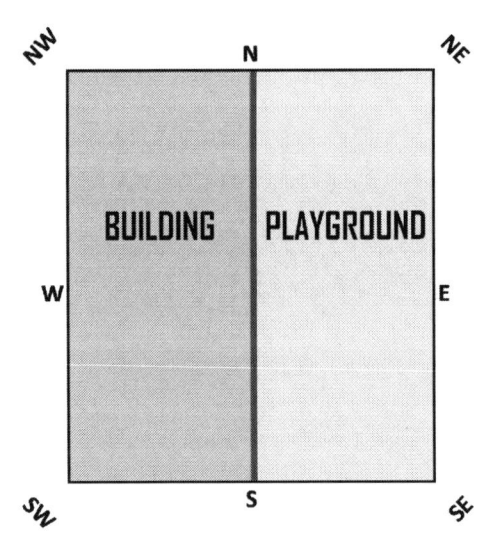

Now, what is the relationship between the playground with Vastu? Which is the best direction for the playground, and why? Let's figure it out.

Divide your entire plot into two halves along the north-south axis. If the maximum part of the playground falls in the East, NE, and North, this school will be successful. If the playground is in the West sector, there are very few possibilities for the school's success.

The playground is nothing but an open area. If the open area is in the East or NE, the building has to be in the West, South, and SW, which is good according to Vastu. We should keep the East, NE, and North as open as possible because they are the origin points of energy. The South, SW, and West have the capability to hold heavy weight, so the building should be in these directions.

It is also a healthy condition if the playground is in the center and the building is on the periphery of the plot. Try to keep the NE as empty as possible in this case as well. We can build a water pool, boring, or submersible in the NE.

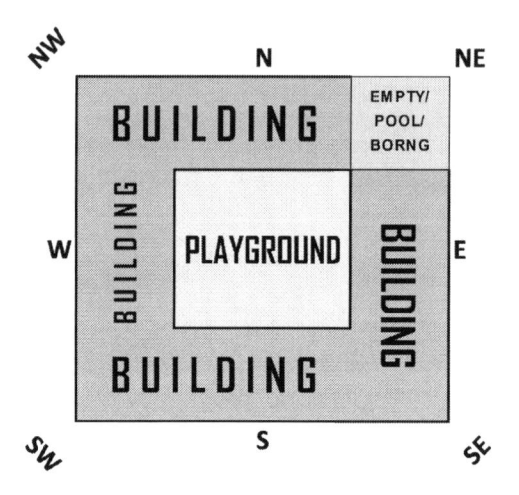

```
         NW              N                NE
         ┌─────────────────────┬──────────┐
         │      BUILDING       │ EMPTY/   │
         │                     │ POOL/    │
         │                     │ BORNG    │
         │  ┌───┬──────────┬───┤          │
         │  │ B │          │ B │          │
       W │  │ U │PLAYGROUND│ U │          │ E
         │  │ I │          │ I │          │
         │  │ L │          │ L │          │
         │  │ D │          │ D │          │
         │  │ I │          │ I │          │
         │  │ N │          │ N │          │
         │  │ G │          │ G │          │
         │  └───┴──────────┴───┘          │
         │      BUILDING                  │
         └────────────────────────────────┘
         SW              S                SE
```

EXTRA IMPORTANT POINTS:

1. In the classroom, students should face toward the East or North, and accordingly, the teacher should face toward the West or South.

2. The principal's office should be in the SW or South.

3. Canteens should be in the SE or NW.

• • • ● • ● • • •

Chapter 3
Vastu for Restaurant

"In the art of arranging spaces, Feng Shui and Vastu speak the language of energy and flow."

Whether a restaurant will be successful or a total loss depends on the key factors affecting its success. Let's find out in this chapter.

The most crucial parts of a restaurant's success are the location of the kitchen and color combinations. The correct direction of the kitchen and the correct direction of the fire/stove can provide immense profit in the restaurant business. I am not saying we can ignore other factors, as they also play a very important role in overall prosperity.

Locations of the kitchen in a restaurant:

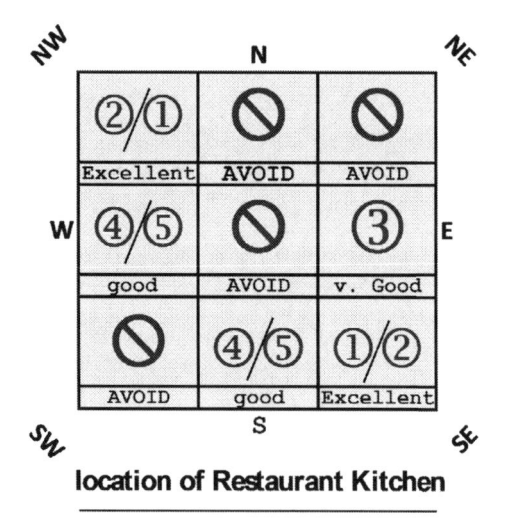

NW	N	NE
②/① Excellent	⊘ AVOID	⊘ AVOID
W ④/⑤ good	⊘ AVOID	③ v. Good E
⊘ AVOID	④/⑤ good	①/② Excellent
SW	S	SE

location of Restaurant Kitchen

This is the same as the location of the kitchen in a residence.

Because it is for a restaurant and we want it to generate profit, it would be better to build the kitchen in the

SE, NW, or E. These three directions are the best. Based on my experience, I suggest you build your restaurant's kitchen in the NW instead of SE because NW is the zone of Air, which is a friend of SE. As we discussed earlier, NW is responsible for bringing guests, and in a restaurant business, all we want are guests. That's why I am considering NW before SE.

If these three locations are not possible, you can choose West and South as the fourth and fifth positions.

It's next to impossible to run a restaurant if you build the kitchen in the North, NE, SW, or center. We have already discussed the kitchen in detail in residential Vastu.

Now let's have a look at color composition:

The best choices are yellow, maroon, and white. You can go with different combinations of these colors. These colors are symbols of success and prosperity and provide a positive ambiance.

For other rooms and utilities, you can refer to "Residential Vastu." or "Master Your Growth With Vastu"

• • • ● • ● • • •

Chapter 4
Vastu For Salons/Parlor

"The beauty of Feng Shui and Vastu lies in their ability to enhance our connection with the environment."

B eauty parlors and unisex salons are in fashion in today's era. Let's design them according to Vastu. Can you guess the key points for these businesses?

The mirror and the wash basin are the key points for the success of a salon. We cannot compromise on the locations of the mirror and wash basin if we want our salon to make a handsome profit. When you visit a new salon, what do you observe at first sight? Mirrors and basins are the major attractions of a salon or parlor. And I don't think you will visit a salon with no mirror.

The best positions to install the mirror and basin are the walls of the NE, east, and north. All other directions must be avoided.

The function of the mirror is to extend the direction in which it is installed. Only the NE, east, and north are beneficial when extended. The extension of other directions is very dangerous and can lead to many problems and losses in the business. Of course, we need to install the basin just below the mirror, as the basin represents the water element. The NE, north, and east also fit perfectly with respect to the water element.

Color composition for a Parlor/salon:

The ideal color is white because it is the color of Venus. This is the best color choice because the driving force of the salon is Venus. You can choose other colors as per your design and theme but try to use white as much as possible.

If you want to sell beauty products in your salon, build the showcase/window/shelf for these products in the NW. This will help to increase the sales of these products."

• • • ● • • ● • • •

Chapter 5
Vastu For Factories

"Good Feng Shui and Vastu create a nurturing environment where dreams can thrive."

It is a thumb rule that your plot has to be in a 90-degree direction. If it is not, you can make it 90 degrees using a pyramid remedy. The applications of Vastu are meaningless if the plot is not on a 90-degree angle.

1. Location of Machinery:

The best location for placing machinery is the southeast (SE), followed by the south and then the west.

NW	N	NE
⑤	⑥	⑧
MEDUIM	MED/LIGHT	AVOID
③ (W)	⑨	⑦ (E)
HEAVY	AVOID	AVOID
①	②	④
HEAVIEST	HEAVIEST	MEDIUM
SW	S	SE

The southwest (SW) and south have the capability to hold heavy weight because they are earth elements. If you have very heavy machinery, you must choose SW or South. The west can also handle weight because it is our back portion, but not as much as SW and south. If you have light or less heavy machinery, you can place it in the west.

The fourth zone is SE, followed by the northwest (NW). You can place medium-heavy machinery in these directions. SE represents our right hand and can hold a reasonable weight. NW is our left hand, which can also hold weight.

The sixth zone is the north, which represents our shoulders and is suitable for medium heavy, and light machinery. You should avoid placing weight in the North because it is the career and money zone.

You should avoid placing machinery in the remaining three zones. But if there is no other possibility, the seventh zone would be the east. Remember that the east represents our chest, and weight on the chest should be avoided.

NE can be used to place light machinery, but it is better to avoid it because it represents our heads, and we should not place weight on our heads.

You must avoid placing machinery in the center because the weight in the center can imbalance all other directions. The center must be open and empty as much as possible.

Simply choose directions according to the weight of your machinery.

Due to any unavoidable reason, if you have to place your machines in the north, east, or northeast, you must follow these principles:

1. Install legs under your machinery to lift them at least 4 inches above the ground. Legs will allow airflow under the heavy machines, making them feel lighter to the earth element.

2. Leave some space between machines and the walls of these zones. There should be at least a 3-4 feet gap. This will also allow energy to flow around the heavy machines.

If you place machinery in the wrong direction, you will face many problems in your business. The machines will frequently malfunction, leading to increased maintenance costs.

• • • • • • • • •

Factories/Raw & Finished Goods

Every factory has a supply of raw material and every factory has to manage an inventory to keep their finished goods. In this chapter, we will learn about the locations to keep our Raw and Finished goods.

Directions for Raw material:

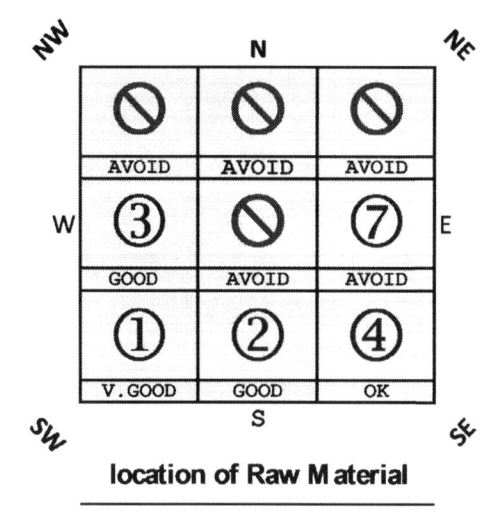

location of Raw Material

Raw material should be considered as weight. So the best directions for this would be according to the directions of weight. It also follows the same logic as the store room because we are essentially storing the raw material in the factory. If you have a large supply of raw material and there are no other options but the prohibited directions (directions to avoid), you can build a platform 3-4 inches above the ground to allow airflow below the material. Don't make this platform with solid material; instead, you can use a net of iron rods or something similar that allows air to pass through it. You may wonder how we can place two different things (machinery and raw materials) in the same location. Don't worry! I will discuss it later.

Directions for finished goods:

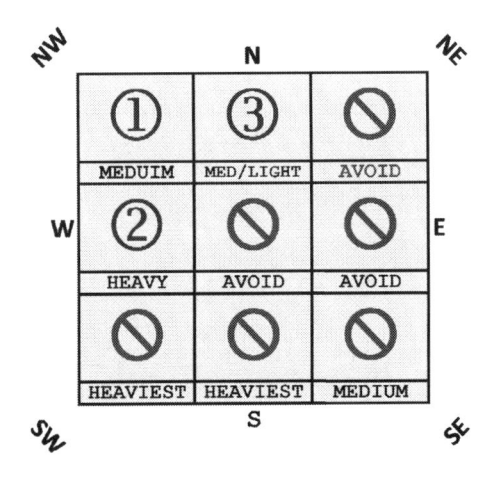

	N	
① MEDUIM	③ MED/LIGHT	🚫 AVOID
② HEAVY	🚫 AVOID	🚫 AVOID
🚫 HEAVIEST	🚫 HEAVIEST	🚫 MEDIUM

(NW, NE, W, E, SW, S, SE as directional markers around the grid)

We want to sell finished goods as fast as possible. Keeping this in mind, the best directions for storing finished goods are as follows:

If you have to keep finished goods in avoided directions, here's what you need to do. Suppose you are keeping goods in an avoided direction. When you receive an order, pick the goods from the northwest (NW), north, or west and fill the empty space with the goods you were keeping in the avoided direction. Don't sell directly from an avoided direction, as it can create an imbalance in the business. Always sell directly from the NW, north, and west, and keep filling the empty space with goods from the impure direction.

• • • • ● • ● • • •

Factories Owner's office

The location of the master bedroom in a house and the location of the owner's office in a commercial building are almost the same, but their importance is different. The master bedroom is more important than the owner's office because the most important thing in a factory is machinery. The importance of the owner's office comes after the machinery. We cannot compromise with the locations of machinery and raw materials, but we can somehow adjust the location of the owner's office according to our needs.

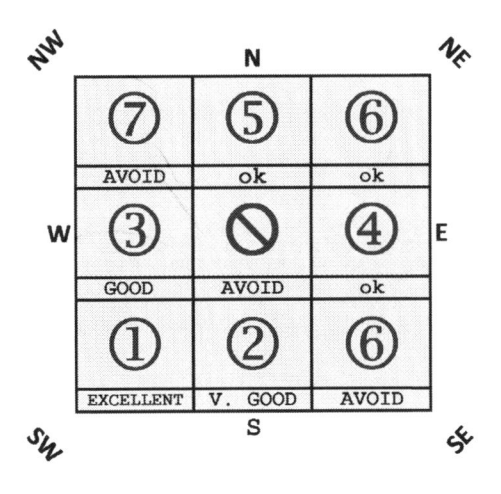

	N	
⑦ AVOID	⑤ ok	⑥ ok
③ GOOD	🚫 AVOID	④ ok
① EXCELLENT	② V. GOOD	⑥ AVOID

(NW top-left, NE top-right, W left, E right, SW bottom-left, S bottom, SE bottom-right)

Undoubtedly, the best location is the southwest (SW), the second-best location is the south, and the third-best location is the west. The east is in fourth place, followed by the north in fifth place, and the northeast (NE) is in sixth place. We should avoid the southeast (SE) and northwest (NW).

The southwest, south, and west have a magnetic force that is good for an office. However, these are also the locations for machinery and raw goods, so how can we fit too many things here? We should always give preference to the machinery first, then give preference to raw goods, and lastly, we can build the office. If there is no space left in a good direction, you can build your office in any other direction according to the sequence order, except for the center.

We should avoid the southeast (SE) because it has a fire element that can irritate the owner at the worksite. The owner may behave rudely with their workers, resulting in problems and losses for the company. We have kept the northwest (NW) for finished goods, so it is also not recommended as a location for the office.

Place the owner's chair so that the owner faces north, east, or northeast (NE). Avoid facing south. Avoid black furniture in the owner's office. The furniture should have legs. There should be a solid wall behind the owner's chair, and windows should be avoided. For better results and extra strength and stability, paste a picture of a solid mountain without water on the wall behind the chair.

If you have multiple floors in your factory, there is no problem. You can utilize different floors for different needs.

• • • • • • • • • •

Location of Boiler

Some factories require boilers, furnaces, or melting areas. Boilers can be categorized into two types: those with chimneys and those without chimneys. Boilers operate at very high temperatures, making them fire elements.

For boilers without chimneys:

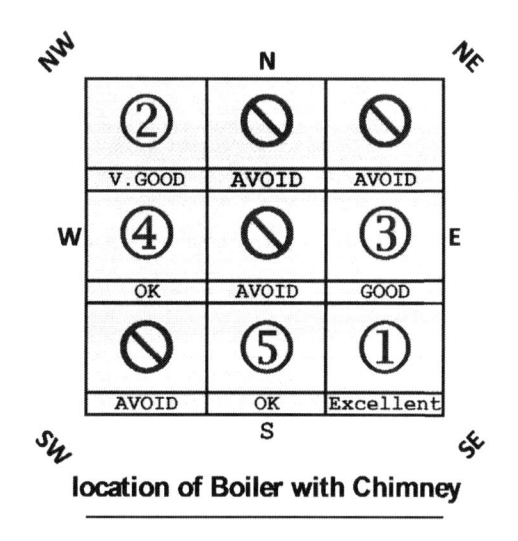

location of Boiler with Chimney

	N	
② V.GOOD	⊘ AVOID	⊘ AVOID
④ OK	⊘ AVOID	③ GOOD
⊘ AVOID	⑤ OK	① Excellent

(NW, NE, W, E, SW, S, SE directions indicated around the grid)

The first zone is SE, followed by NW and East. SE and East are fire zones, while NW is an air zone. I strongly advise against compromising these zones, but if it's not possible to accommodate all three, West and South can serve as the fourth and fifth zones. It is permissible to construct boilers in the West because, as mentioned earlier, it is the parliament zone and is compatible with almost everything. According to feng shui, the south is the fire zone, which is why we have placed it in the fifth position. Other directions should be avoided. The north is associated with money, so placing fire there is not recommended. NE is the zone of prosperity, hence fire should not be placed there. Fire in the center can disrupt the benefits in all directions. SW is the zone of strength and stability, and fire can potentially destroy it. If your furnace is already located in the wrong direction, I suggest relocating the furnace or boiler to a more favorable direction instead of relying on remedies.

Boilers with chimneys:

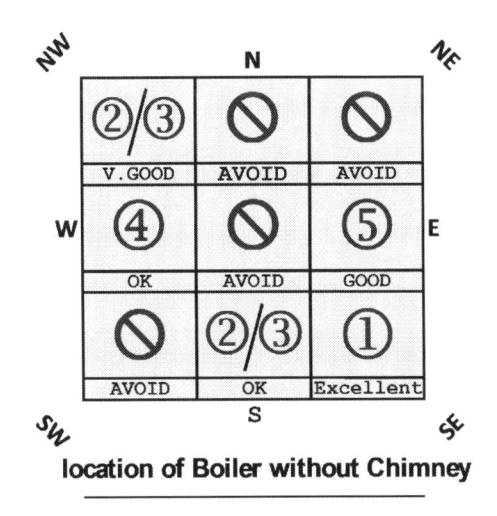

NW	N	NE
②/③ V.GOOD	🚫 AVOID	🚫 AVOID
④ OK (W)	🚫 AVOID	⑤ GOOD (E)
🚫 AVOID	②/③ OK	① Excellent
SW	S	SE

location of Boiler without Chimney

This configuration involves fire, as well as height and weight due to the presence of the chimney. The recommended sequence for the best locations is SE, NE, or South, West, and East. South is capable of supporting weight and is also the fire zone according to feng shui. NW is an air zone that complements fire and can handle weight and height. East is ranked fifth because it can handle fire but not necessarily height and weight. The explanations for other directions can be carried from the above-mentioned considerations.

• • • ● • ● • • •

Chapter 6

Vastu For Gym

"A well-balanced home brings harmony to the mind, body, and spirit."

The gym has become a basic requirement for today's youth. Everyone wants a fit and muscular body, which is beneficial for health. This increased the demand for gyms, and we can observe gyms in almost every locality of any city. In this chapter, we are going to learn about the key points of gym Vastu.

The most crucial things for a gym's success are the fitness equipment (i.e., treadmill, dumbbells, and other machinery). All gym equipment is usually heavy. While designing the Vastu, we consider them as weight. The locations for gym equipment are similar to the locations of machinery in a factory.

You should place all heavy equipment in the SW, South, and West because these directions are capable of holding heavy weights.

For medium-weight equipment, you should go with the SE and NW.

Adjust the positioning of the equipment in such a way that the user is facing towards the North or East while using the equipment. Avoid them facing South and West.

Gyms also have mirrors. As we discussed earlier, the best locations for the mirrors are NE, East, and North. The directions of the mirror are uncompromisable.

Color combination for the gym:

White, maroon, blue, and green are ideal choices. You must avoid black as the color of your gym."

• • • ● ● • ● • • •

Chapter 7
Vastu for Boutique

"The power of Feng Shui and Vastu lies in their ability to transform a house into a home filled with positive vibrations."

The boutique is basically the place/shop where ladies sell garments. In this chapter we will learn about the position of garments, trial room, show windows, and mannequin position of the tailor and the color combination.

- There are lots of **stocks** in your boutique but there must be a special article you want to sell in maximum numbers because it is most profitable. If you want to sell goods in high quantity you must place them in NW, West, and North.

- You should install your **show windows** and mannequins in SW and south.

- **The owner's/manager's/cashier's counter** should be in SW and South and the face should be towards north or east.

- The best location for the **Trail room** is in the West followed by the south and SW. SE can be considered at last. Avoid NE East and NE. and we very well that the mirror of the trial room will go on the walls of North, east, and NE.

- **Location of Tailor:** best and ideal locations are South and SE because the tailor works with scissors and a sewing machine, Mars is considered a machine operator in the zone of Mars

South.

Color combinations:

The ideal color for your boutique is **Green and white**, try to keep Green as dominant as possible because it is the color of Mercury providing balance and prosperity and white is the color of Venus which is helpful in this business.

If you follow all these things correctly it will propel your business.

• • • ● • ● • • •

Chapter 8
Vastu for Petrol Pump

"When you align your space with Feng Shui and Vastu, you align yourself with the universe."

Have you ever thought that Vastu can be applied to petrol pumps?

The key point of the petrol pump is the pits for the storage of petrol. The petrol pump stores petrol in underground tanks, which are further supplied to your vehicle with the help of a pump. We already know which directions allow us to dig. The NE, East, and North are the directions in which we can create a pit. If the pits/tanks of your petrol pump are in the appropriate position, it will be a successful petrol pump. But if the pits are in the SW, SE, or South, the business will result in a total loss. I have seen many petrol pumps built in an extremely good location, but they are not doing well because they have built their pits in the wrong direction.

The West and NW are not-so-good, not-so-bad type directions for pits. You can choose these directions as your last option.

Boring, owner's cabins, toilets, and other things should also be built according to Vastu.

Many people think that south-facing petrol pumps are bad and north-facing ones are good, but this is not true. I never believe that north-facing or south-facing can be good or bad; it always depends on various factors. If you observe petrol pumps, you will find that south-facing petrol pumps are doing great while north-facing ones are having trouble. Let me explain why: petrol tanks are installed in locations where public vehicles usually don't come, due to safety precautions. If the petrol pump is south-facing, vehicles would be entering from the south, which means we have to build the tank in the north. This condition is automatically according to Vastu. If the petrol pump is north-facing, the tank would be in the south, and this condition is against Vastu principles."

• • • • • • • • • •

Chapter 9
Vastu for Hospitals

"Feng Shui and Vastu remind us that our living spaces have the power to shape our lives."

The key points for a hospital are ICU, OT, OPD, etc. because these are the pillars of a hospital's reputation. The entire success of a hospital is situated in these three departments. The lower the mortality rate, the more reputed the hospital is.

The best location for ICU and OT is the East, followed by the North, NE, and finally the West. The East is the purest zone and the sector of health. The NE is the purest direction but still ranked third because we want minimum construction in the NE. During the operation, blood droplets, pus, waste bandages, and used cotton pieces fall on the floor, which is like throwing impurities in the purest direction. The West is an impure direction but still a good direction for ICU and OT because, as I mentioned earlier, the West is like a parliamentary zone. And the energy flow is from East to West, so we can align the patient's bed with the flow of energy.

OT and ICU must be avoided in the South and SW, as these are the directions of Yama and Rahu-Ketu, the most impure directions. These zones are dangerous for patients.

NW should also be avoided for OT and ICU because it is the zone of air. If the airflow is slow, it is good, but if it is too fast, it can transform into a dangerous tornado.

For OPD, which is the zone where patients come, consult the doctor, and leave, the best direction would be NW, followed by the North and West.

Color combination:

The dominating color for hospitals is yellow. Always go with yellow or shades of yellow. This is the color of Jupiter, who is the Guru of Gods. This color represents healing.

For doctors' cabins, the best directions are SW, West, and South."

Chapter 10
Vastu for Cinema Hall & Theatre

"A well-designed space can inspire, energize, and uplift the human spirit. That's the magic of Feng Shui and Vastu."

You may have guessed it right! The key point of the cinema is its screen. The best directions to install the screen are NE, East, and North. We want the viewers to face these directions while they are enjoying the movie. Seats in the theater are arranged on a slope. The first row of seats is at the lowest level, and the last row is above all so that viewers in the last row can see the screen clearly. For better prosperity and success, the slope should be towards the NE, East, and North.

The ticket window should be in the NW, West, or North. This configuration will increase ticket sales.

Chapter 11
Vastu for Banquet Halls

"In the realm of Feng Shui and Vastu, every corner and element holds a story waiting to be told."

The key point for an indoor banquet hall is its stage. The ideal locations for the stage are the SW, South, and West. We must avoid the NE, East, and North. The more elevated and robust the SW, South, and West are, the more beneficial it is. This quality of these directions makes them perfect for a stage.

Toilets, staircases, kitchens, and other facilities should also be designed according to Vastu.

In large banquet halls, there are separate halls for starters, the main course, and coffee. These halls should be built in the SW, South, and West. We must avoid building them in the NE, East, and North."

Chapter 12
Vastu for Jewelry Shops

"Feng Shui and Vastu teach us to live in harmony with our surroundings, creating a sense of balance and well-being."

The key points for a jewelry shop are the safe, mirror, and owner's seating. The safe should be in the SW, South, or West. These three zones are the best because they represent stability. We must avoid placing the safe in the NW, SE, East, and North. The SE is a direction that is neither good nor bad, but it is not preferable for the safe.

As we have already discussed, mirrors should be installed in the North, East, and NE. Installing mirrors in all other directions must be avoided.

While sitting in the shop and dealing with customers, the owner should face the NE, East, or North. These directions are considered the purest, providing the owner with pure energy throughout the day."

• • • • • • • • • •

Chapter 13
Vastu For Shops

"When we embrace Feng Shui and Vastu, we invite positive energies to flow and transform our lives."

This chapter is for all kinds of shops. For example grocery stores, utility shops, clothing shops, chemist shops, hardware shops, etc. Here are some important key points for shops:

1. Owner's seating:

- If the shop is south-facing, the owner should sit in the SW.

- If the shop is west-facing, the owner should sit in the SW.

- If the shop is north-facing, the owner should sit in the North or NE.

- If the shop is east-facing, the owner should sit in the East or NE.

- If the shop is NE-facing, the owner should sit in the North.

- If the shop is SE-facing, the owner should sit in the South.

- If the shop is NW-facing, the owner should sit in the West.

- If the shop is SW-facing, the owner should sit in the South.

2. Important stock:

The stock that the shopkeeper wants to sell in large quantities should be kept in the NW, North, and West.

3. Cash box:

Keep the cash box in such a manner that when you open it, it opens towards the North, East, or NE. If this is not possible, use cash boxes with lids so that you can open them directly upwards. The cash box should never open towards the South and SW.

4. Temple:

The temple should be built or installed in the NE, East, and North.

5. Color combination:

The color of the shop should be white or off-white. Avoid dark colors.

Do not place any goods in the center of the shop.

The main gate of the shop should also be according to Vastu, as we have already discussed in one of the previous chapters.

Chapter 14
Factory Location of ETP

"Feng Shui and Vastu are gateways to understanding the interplay between our external and internal environments."

The requirement for an Effluent Treatment Plant (ETP) is not known to many people. An ETP is used in many factories where there is a need for a large amount of water. The government cannot provide that much water to the factories as they also have to supply it to the residents. That's why we use ETPs to recycle water in factories. Since there is a large presence of water, we will determine its directions according to the water element. Digging is also required to build a tank for water storage. Therefore, the ideal directions for an ETP are similar to the directions for boring, underground tanks, submersibles, etc.

The best directions are northeast (NE), east, and north. All other directions are not advisable.

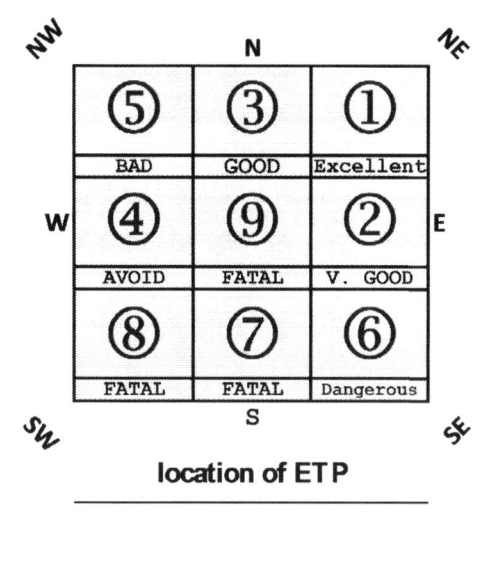

⑤ BAD	③ GOOD	① Excellent
④ AVOID	⑨ FATAL	② V. GOOD
⑧ FATAL	⑦ FATAL	⑥ Dangerous

location of ETP

Chapter 15
Factories Location of Servant Quarters

"A space that honors the principles of Feng Shui and Vastu becomes a sacred place that nurtures the soul."

Many factories have to build servant quarters for their workers to stay. So let's see the best and ideal locations for these quarters.

	N	
🚫 AVOID	🚫 AVOID	🚫 AVOID
② V. GOOD	🚫 AVOID	③ OK
🚫 AVOID	🚫 AVOID	① Excellent

location of Servant Quarters

The best location is southeast (SE). Our shastra (scripture) also suggests the same. In old times, rich people wanted their servants to wake up and finish most of the work before they themselves woke up. The reason behind choosing this location was that the Sun rises in the East and reaches the SE in about an hour. If we build a room in the SE, sunrays will enter the room early in the morning and the servant will wake up. From today's point of view, we can explain it like this - the SE is a very energetic zone because it is a fire zone, and this will fill the worker with energy, making them more productive. If you can afford to make a room for your servant, you can also select this direction for your home.

If the SE is not possible, the next best location is the West. The West is the zone of stability, and this will make the servant loyal, trustworthy, and compatible with you.

The third-best zone is the east.

You must avoid these rooms/quarters in the southwest (SW) and south. Doing so can be very dangerous as these are the zones of the owner. The servant may try to become the owner and may become jealous of you.

Also, avoid the northwest (NW), north, and northeast (NE).

• • • • • • • • • •

Conclusion

Congratulations!

You have come to the end of this book. A vast majority of the readers don't finish the book, but you did, so you deserve a pat on your back. I hope it was a good journey and hope you have a smile on your face as you are reading this final page of the book. After all, I was trying to build a Successful Destiny throughout this book.

I wish you a splendid life full of happiness and fulfillment.

Cheers,
Sooraj Achar

· · · ● · ● · · ·

May I Ask You for a Small Favor?

At the outset, I want to give you a big thanks for taking out time to read this book. You could have chosen any other book, but you chose mine, and I totally appreciate this.

I hope you got at least a few actionable insights that will have a positive impact on your day-to-day life.

Can I ask for 30 seconds more of your time?

I would love it if you could leave a review about the book. Reviews may not matter to big-name authors; but they're a tremendous help for authors like me, who don't have much following. They help me to grow my readership by encouraging folks to take a chance on my books.

To put it straight, reviews are the lifeblood of any author.

Please leave your review by scanning the below **QR Code**. It will directly lead you to the book review page.

Or visit the **"Reviews Section"** of this book's page on Amazon.

It will just take less than a minute of your time, but will tremendously help me to reach out to more people, so please leave your review.

SOORAJ ACHAR

Thanks for your support of my work. And I would love to see your review.

• • • ● • ● • • •

Preview of My Best Selling Books

Numerology Mastery Series

★ **Why do 80% of People Fail to Recognize their True Potential ??**

This **Self-Help** book will help you **Recognize, Transform and Navigate** your life toward a **Happier Destiny**.

I always say that your **Date of Birth** is so precious. God has placed many diamonds on your date of birth you are not aware of. It doesn't matter if your date of birth is good or bad. The idea is how you can take the best out of your date of birth. **Psychology of Numbers** is a perfect, **complete beginner's guide** for those who are new to numerology.

★ What Role Does Numerology Play in Your Life?

- You have been surrounded by numbers since the day you were Born. Now use them to unlock your Destiny.

- Wherever you go in your life, the numbers always move on with you.

- When you are born, on the very first day of your life, you get your date of birth, which is made up of numbers.

- When you get admitted to school, you get your roll number.

- When you get your results, you get a percentage of numbers.

- When you get a job, you get a salary and EMP-ID number.

- When you buy any vehicle, it has a number plate.

- When you travel, you get a ticket and seat number

- When you check into a hotel, you get a room number.

- When you want to call a person, you have to dial numbers.

- When you get married, there is also a date attached to it.

- If there is Life, there are Numbers. You cannot get rid of Numbers.

★ Your **Name Spelling** also plays an important role according to your date of birth. Believe me or not, **30%**

to 40% of your success or failure depends on your name spelling. If you keep your name spelling correct, you can achieve 30% to 40% more success in your life.

♥ Psychology of Numbers will help you...

✓ Recognize Your Strengths and Weaknesses.

✓ Find Your Lucky Numbers and Colours.

✓ Correct Your Name Spelling without changing your documents.

✓ Choose the Right Profession.

✓ Find a Compatible Life-Partner.

✓ With Simple Remedies for All Your Problems.

✓ Check Your Foreign or Abroad Opportunities.

✓ Predict your Future Years, Months, and Days of importance, which helps you take Better Decisions.

✓ Understand the Behavioral Patterns of People Around You.

✓ Transform and Navigate your life for a Better Future.

★ If you are ready to make a commitment to yourself that you want to learn everything that is presented to you, then it is our commitment to you that this will surely help you a lot. There is no reason why this book will not change your destiny or transform your future. But, there is an important thing you must keep in mind, i.e., **"You will bring this change through TRANSFORMATION, not through MIRACLES"**.

★ If you learn **Numerology**, then

(a) "You will be **awakened**", which makes it likely to "**transform**" your life.

(b) Ultimately, "You will be able to **navigate** your life".

★ Life is all about "**Awakening**,", "**Transformation**," and eventually, "Knowing How To **Navigate** It?"

★ Order **Psychology of Numbers** now to make the most of your **Health, Relationships, Career, and Money** by unlocking the **Power of Numbers**.

Check Out My Best Selling Books Here

Numerology Mastery Series

1. Psychology of Numbers Vol-1

2. Psychology of Numbers Vol-2

Vastu Mastery Series

★ **How Can These Books Work Miracles in Your Life?**

This Self-Help Book is A Perfect Blueprint Describing Ancient Principles for Modern Living. A Step-by-step Practical Guide for Beginners to Creating a Positive Living Space and for Optimal Well-Being.

Learn:

★ **How to Implement Feng-Shui/Vastu in your Day-to-Day Life !!**

★ **What Role Do Feng-Shui and Vastu Play in Your Life?**

★ **Relationship between Vastu and Feng-Shui?**

Vastu is used to Diagnose, and Feng Shui is the Remedy. Vastu is used to identify the disease, and Feng Shui is the medicine. Vastu and Feng Shui are complementary to each other.

Vastu Shastra is an Ancient Indian Science of architecture and construction, which is based on the principles of harmony and balance between humans and their environment. The main focus of Vastu is to create a harmonious balance between the 5-Elements of nature, i.e., Earth, Water, Air, Fire, & Space. It emphasizes on directions and orientation and uses various elements like colors, shapes, and materials to create a balance and positive energy in the living spaces.

Feng Shui, on the other hand, is a Chinese Philosophical System of harmonizing everyone with the surrounding environment. It is based on the principles of Qi (Chi), the life force that flows through all living things, and Yin and Yang, the balance of opposite forces. Feng Shui focuses on the placement of objects, furniture, and structures in living spaces to optimize the flow of energy, or "Qi." It also considers the orientation of the building, the placement of doors and windows, and the use of colors, shapes, & materials to create balance & harmony.

In summary, both Vastu and Feng Shui aim to create balance and harmony in living spaces, but Vastu is more focused on directions and orientation, while Feng Shui emphasizes the flow of energy & balance of opposing forces.

★ **The Benefits of Reading This Book Include:**

✓ **Health and Well-Being:** Vastu principles aim to create a harmonious and balanced environment that can promote physical, mental, and emotional well-being.

✓ **Financial Prosperity:** Vastu principles are believed to help attract positive energy and good fortune, leading to financial prosperity.

✓ **Improved Relationships:** Vastu principles can help create an atmosphere of peace and harmony, which can lead to improved relationships with family, friends, & colleagues.

✓ **Increased Productivity:** A Vastu-compliant environment is said to be conducive to productivity and efficiency, leading to greater success in personal & professional life.

✓ **Spiritual Growth:** Vastu principles are based on ancient Vedic knowledge and aim to promote spiritual growth & enlightenment.

✓ **Enhanced Creativity:** Vastu principles are believed to enhance creativity and inspiration, which can be beneficial for artists, writers, & other creative professionals.

✓ **Better Sleep Quality:** Vastu principles can help create a peaceful and relaxing environment, which can improve the quality of sleep and help reduce stress & anxiety.

✓ **Improved Mental Clarity:** A Vastu-compliant environment is said to help clear the mind and improve mental clarity, which can be beneficial for decision-making & problem-solving.

✓ **Enhanced Career Prospects:** Vastu principles can help align one's career goals with their personal strengths and abilities, leading to greater career success & satisfaction.

★ Overall, the benefits of Vastu can contribute to a more Balanced, Harmonious, & Fulfilling Life.

★ Order "Master Your DESTINY With Vastu" now to make the most of your Health, Relationships, Career, & Money by unlocking the Power of Directions.

Check Out My Best Selling Books Here

3. Master Your DESTINY With Vastu

4. Master Your GROWTH With Vastu

5. Master Your WEALTH With Vastu

Testimonials

These are a few feedbacks from my clients across different parts of the world. Kindly go through their reviews to understand how Numerology and Vastu helped them.

1. Ekta Gupta – Kolkata, India

"2021 is a difficult year for me. I have consulted a few numerologists. I have received vague answers and complicated solutions. I'm new to numerology. Charges were expensive. Sooraj is a good and kind soul. He is very patient with me. He answered all my

questions. I had 1000 questions. More ever he helped me to find a business name with no extra charges. I'm grateful to him. With your help, I'm sorted out with my business name. I had a lot of anxiety about it. I'm confident now. Sooraj is a helpful soul. He is patient and explains if one has questions. He doesn't rush into closing the job. You can consult him easily. I am going to recommend him to newbies like me. He is not going to cheat you or misguide you".

2. Neetu Ganglani - Stanley, Hongkong

"Hello Sooraj, I can't thank you enough. At the age of 45, I could find an ideal life partner for myself. And my compatibility with the boy I like. Got to know our strengths and weaknesses. Your suggestions helped me to *find the right life partner. You have a bright future. Good luck"*

3. Lensly Kwaimani - Solomon Islands, Oceania

"Dear friend, glad I came across you. My daughter Felinda Kwaimani is sick for a long time and I was very much worried. Thank you for giving suggestions and guidance".

4. Seham Shabhir - Talagang, Pakistan

"You're one of the best numerologists...your predictions are correct...you are a very humble person...you gave answers to all of my questions in detail ... I'm very thankful to you. Ur remedies prove very helpful for me. He is the very best numerologist... I recommend him for all.. u should consult him to get

rid of your problems..his remedies work like a magic"

5. Naveen Kumar - Bengaluru, India

"Sooraj is a gem as a human and as a professional. Before approaching Sooraj, I have enquired and got inputs from other numerologists and I did some research as well. I Was not satisfied with the answers provided by them and most of them were behind fees, even after paying for the consultation they charge extra for clarifying doubts. However, Sooraj was awesome in client satisfaction and the way he follows up with the client for providing suggestions. He takes the initiative to follow up and provide the best solutions and describes the reason for the input. I definitely suggest Sooraj to anyone who is looking for start-up business names or anything relat-

ed to numerology. He has a good amount of knowledge and patience to answer all my queries".

6. Sneha S - Karnataka, India

"Hi Sooraj, it's a great prediction starting from Personality Traits to our Abroad Opportunities to future achievements. Everything is perfectly predicted with correct proof and explanations which help us to understand our lives better and take steps accordingly to numerology. Everyone are curious to know more about their life just to know when, how & what situations they will come across and how they need to overcome everything. Thanks a lot, Sooraj, for the best Numerology Prediction which helped us to understand ourselves better".

7. Aditya S - Mumbai, India

"Sooraj, your numerology predictions are brilliant and accurate. Your Suggestions helped me find out whether my current job is suitable for me or not. I would suggest people consult you in due course of time".

8. Nabanita M - West Bengal, India

"Hi Sooraj, it's helpful and gives me a quick idea and help. Thank you so much for being there. It helped me to understand my situation It helps in my career and marriage. The information is good".

9. Naresh – Bangalore, India

"Hello Sooraj, it was satisfactory. Can decide further based on the info shared & also can see positive outcomes looking forward to checking how it works".

10. Harishchandra Dnyaneshwar Deshmukh – Delhi, India

"Hi sir, Padhai puri nahi kar paya, 11 k salary he, Stable nahi hu life me, Business success nahi milta. Thank u sir for sharing my report and helping me understand my strengths and weaknesses".

Author Profile

Follow my **Author Profile Page** to get updates on all my books: **https://amazon.com/author/sooraj_achar**

Grab your **Free Gift** if you missed it: **https://sooraj.sooraj-achar.com/free-gift**

Please Leave Your **Valuable Review** here: **https://relinks.me/B0BXX3WZY3**

For 1-to-1 consultation, scan the **QR code** or contact: **info@sooraj-achar.com**

Follow **Author's BookBub** Profile: **https://www.bookbub.com/authors/sooraj-achar**

Stay Connected to our below **Social Media Handles**:

https://amzn.to/3CgQHF9

https://medium.com/@soorajachar99

https://bit.ly/3M7gIu2

instagram.com/psychology_of_numberz/

https://bit.ly/3dO6aDh

https://bit.ly/3LXBTyz

https://bit.ly/3E9vKxc

• • • • • • • • •

Disclaimer

This book is for entertainment purposes only. Readers acknowledge that the author does not render legal, financial, medical, or professional advice. The content within this book has been derived from various sources. Please consult a licensed professional before attempting any techniques outlined in this book.

By reading this document, the reader agrees that under no circumstances is the author responsible for any direct or indirect losses incurred as a result of the use of the information contained within this document, including but not limited to errors, omissions, or inaccuracies. Adherence to all applicable laws and regulations, including international, federal, state, and local governing professional licensing, business practices, advertising, and all other jurisdiction, is the sole responsibility of the purchaser or reader. Neither the author nor the publisher assumes any responsibility or liability whatsoever on behalf of the purchaser or reader of these materials. Any perceived slight of any individual or organization is purely unintentional.

• • • • • • • • • •

Could You Please Leave A Review On The Book?

One Last Time!

I'd love it if you could leave a review about the book. Reviews may not matter to big-name authors; but they're a tremendous help for authors like me, who don't have much following. They help me to grow my readership by encouraging folks to take a chance on my books.

To put it straight– reviews are the lifeblood of any author.

Please leave your review by clicking the below link, it will directly lead you to the book review page.

It will just take less than a minute of yours, but will tremendously help me to reach out to more people, so please leave your review.

Thank you for supporting my work and I'd love to see your review of the book.

• • • • • • • • • •

Printed in Great Britain
by Amazon

8ec4cfc5-ce77-4628-ba50-eab349f4b329R01